With Every Sense, I Love You

"My Spidey Senses Are Tingling"

Lillian Carrington

Bookleaf
Publishing

India | USA | UK

Made with ❤ on the BookLeaf Publishing Platform
www.bookleafpub.in
www.bookleafpub.com

Dedication

To the me who dared to feel deeply,
the me who stumbled through the shadows,
the me who stood tall in her light,
the me who persevered —
Thank you.

Thank you for holding on
when hope was just a whisper,
for gathering every shattered piece
and weaving them back together.

This book is for you —
for the quiet strength behind the pain,
for the love that slowly found its way home,
and for the promise of every tomorrow yet to come.

Preface

This book is the warmth I never thought I'd feel again. The warmth I finally feel from the light at the end of the tunnel. It is the proof that even after you weathered the storm, you can bloom and your heart can blossom. For a long time, I lived inside the ache — learning what it meant to let go, to break, to rebuild, to remember how to hold myself gently.

But these pages? They are the sunrise. They are the breath after the crying stops. They are the love I found — first in myself, and then, slowly, all around me. If you're holding this book, maybe you're somewhere between the breaking and the blooming too. I hope these words remind you — there is beauty in the becoming. And the light will always find its way back to you.

"There is a crack in everything, that's how the light gets in." - Leonard Cohen

Acknowledgements

To every version of me who made it here — thank
you. This book would not exist without your quiet
strength. To the hands I once held, and the ones I
let go of — thank you for teaching me what love is,
and what it is not.

To the silence, the soft mornings,
the late nights filled with writing and remembering
— thank you for your patience.
To the ink, the pages, the stillness — you carried
the weight when I could not.
You made art from ache, and turned silence into
something sacred.

And finally, to love itself —
thank you for returning to me. In words, in people,
in *Spirit*.
I am no longer searching.
I am *Home.*

Kissed Back to Life

Lips touch for the first time
Suddenly I'm coming to
The light shining in my eyes
Fresh air hitting my nose
Lungs filling up with air
I breath out oxygen
Never knowing I stopped taking it in
Darkness surrounded me
Long enough I never knew the difference
Like I was living in a waking coma
Body was once cold and numb
Now is sweaty and burning up
Heart is beating again
Stronger than it ever has been before
My vision is clear, my mind is sharp
His lips saved me from drowning
In my own dreaded despair
I didn't realize I was slipping
Puzzle pieces returning to me
Ones I didn't even realize were missing

At First Touch

I'm melting
At the touch of his hand
Each touch and trace
Worries fade
Peace sets in
I fall a bit harder
Enamored by his soft gentle touch
Fascinated like the slow careful stroke of pen

Whispers of a Softer Love

Talked to be heard
Softened to be seen
Opened up to be held
Reality sets the scene
Trust above all else
Suddenly life is so serene
Connection deeper than ever
Communication clearer than water

Higher Love

Floating as I gaze into his eyes
Mesmerized by the light
True love raining down
A divine intervention
Orchestrated by a higher power
Universe as the conductor
Invisible strings at play
Crossed paths in divine union
Aura's shining the way
Lighting the path
Fate handled the math

Keen Eyes

You saw me in a way
I've never been seen before
Allowed me to see parts of myself
I hid from the world, believed were buried
You loved pieces of me
I thought were broken
You weren't scared or taken back
Of the possibility of getting cut
You showed me I can be seen
Even when I'm not in view
I can be heard in my silence
I can breathe when my lungs feel stuck

Ears Of Gold

I'm one of one
This I've always known
Since I was born, I always felt alone
I'm used to holding space for others
Offering a listening ear
A shoulder to cry on
I'm not used to taking up space
Since for the longest time
I just felt like a waste of it
I do my best to make others feel wanted
I do my best and I do what I can
I lend a helping hand
Never knew I'd be touched
By a healing hand
He holds space for me for hours
Listening intently, holding me ever so gently
Feels quite uncomfortable
Like I've finally been released of these chains
Not used to this feeling
Like I'm experiencing growing pains

True Sight

I told myself that I wanted to be seen fully
Yet it never occurred to me how exposed I'd feel
Like I'm face to face with my childhood bully
As if I'm standing under a spotlight
But I stare back at myself in the mirror
No one was harder on me than myself
I see myself truly, never been clearer
I can't hide, I know that won't last long
Sweating under his gaze, his eyes study me
Like I'm under a magnifying glass
No longer flinch at my own reflection
Finally finding my way out of this maze
I've passed my own inspection

Put Back Together in Color

From as far back as I can remember
Grey skies, dark clouds hung above me
My once colorful outer expression
Drained into a lifeless depression
Along the way I picked apart my past
I dissected the wrongs placed upon me
Righted the ones I played a part in
I infected myself with negative self talk
Draining my self esteem
Deflating my self confidence
I wasn't the best version of myself
I never let myself forget that part
I picked myself up piece by piece
Not forcing myself back together
Held myself gently with compassion

My dark clouds started to move
The damp skies turned from grey
To a symphony of all the colors
No rain = no rainbow
Without my downfall,
I never would have risen
Without the tears,
I never would've grown
Without the lessons,
I would've never learned
Had I not started my healing journey;
I could've missed this golden opportunity
Knocking on my heart
Love asking to be let in
My Soul returning home

Where My Pieces Fit

Something has clicked
Another piece of the puzzle
Has just been revealed
Found its place in the picture
I finally feel wanted and picked
A happy ending; I couldn't predict
Feels like a fairytale, that I can admit

The Way Back to Love

Knew my heart was hardened
Since I met him it's started to soften
Followed my heart at each and every turn
Listened to my intuition above all else
No longer fighting the inevitable
I surrender to this fated encounter

The Taste of Hope

Kissing him is like
Swimming in the deep end
Afraid I don't ever want to come up for air
Submerging myself in his presence
Feeding the flame afraid I'll overheat
Careful to not smother the fire
His hands engulf my being
And they cool me down
His patience calms my body
Learning to love again
Is like he's teaching me to swim
Going over the basics and fundamentals
Capturing these momento occasions on film
Synchronized swimmers like we're *Elemental* lovers

Lovesick

What's Scarier Than Falling in Love?
I fear I'll fall and break my own heart
If I'm being truly honest, truth is
I don't fear that I'll fall in love with you
The real fear is that I know I already have
I fear I could break my own heart before
ever giving you the chance to hold it
I fear that I could end up loving you
more than I could ever love myself
I fear I could crash and burn my world
just to get a glimpse into yours
I fear I could break two hearts
in the process of protecting one
I fear I could abandon ship before
you ever have the chance to board
I fear I've fallen in love with someone
that I don't see myself ever falling out with
I fear I've fallen in love, with the love of my life
But I fear the what if; what if it isn't our time yet?

Found in the Falling Apart

Walls crumbling down beside me
Roof caving in all around me
The house I once knew
Is now laying on top of me
The world I once lived in
Is crashing down while I'm crashing out
The me that once stood tall
Has fallen

Cupid's Calling

Grew comfortable in my walls being down
There was no real threat to my heart
Now that there is, my walls are growing
Just as fast as this love is flowing
I thought someone was knocking
But turns out it was an arrow
Being shot into my heart
Time did its part
Walls can't keep him out
Sees me like he has x-ray vision
Help! There's been a collision
He's struck my heart with such precision
Eyes closed, I can still make this decision
A love story I couldn't possibly envision

Beyond

We communicate without words
We converse through our senses
A mutual exchange through music
Feeling the beat, humming the tune
Both wondering if it's too soon
We let our intuition do the talking
While our hearts do the walking
In sync as a needle and thread
Seamlessly moving together
Stringing together a web of fate
It can't be explained in words
It's something only we know
Don't hold one another back
Encourage each other to grow
Like a secret recipe we cracked
A hidden fortress we stumbled upon

The end of a rainbow we found
Made our own pot to piss in
Golden hour of magic, luck and trust
Wasn't a game of tag, no chasing
A matter of gardening, to attract
Butterflies admired, flying freely
Floating as daintily as clouds do
The feeling in my belly is bubbly
Not nerves, no anxiety, not fear
Simply soul-full contentment
He gets me like no other
He sees me like no one else
We're two shooting stars
Aligning in the night sky
Paths crossed multiple times
Destined to meet
Meant to be

My Heart Knows The Way

My body knew before I did
I knew when my cheeks hurt
from smiling and laughing
When they no longer stung from crying
I knew when I felt wide awake
after a sleepless night
I knew when I cried in front of him
for the first time he simply listened
I knew when he didn't tell me
it would be okay but that *I* would be
I knew when I left with more
energy than I came in with
I knew when he remembered
what I wore the first time we met
I knew when I slept better at his
house than I ever did mine
I knew when he saw past my body
and grabbed ahold of my *Soul*
I knew when the butterflies never came
yet the feeling never left

The Scent of New Love

One of a kind, smells divine
High on his smell
Addicted to his scent
Sent from the heavens above
Always has me screaming out
His scent draws me in
Catch a whiff and I'm entranced
His aura is a bright fire
His essence is the igniter
Attracting me like a pied piper
Not sure I can feel any lighter
Suddenly my past is imploding
A *volcano* of love has erupted
My capacity to love is exploding
I know him to be near
In this *wilderness* of Tender Love & Care
I sense his scent miles away
Just like a bloodhound
Spellbound by what we found
Never met such a *Gentle-Man*

Green Lights Only

Love isn't a race or marathon
But I'm still trying to pace myself
The caution tape wrapped around my heart
Was no match for his warm, gentle touch
Didn't even ask me to remove it
Never needed my worth to prove it
All the signs point to yes
All my senses know it to be true
Love is trickier the second time around
You know the risks, the pain, the danger
My body knows
My heart wants to hide
My mind has started to run
It can't make sense of this perfect equation
It has no job in a perfect world
My mind's not ready to accept the obvious
It doesn't feel safe yet
Since there was a crash in my past
Feels eerie
My mind is foggy

My heart left weary
Like the scene hasn't been cleared yet
My heart is leading the way
My body is running right behind
Where my mind is still trying to tie
the laces of my velcro sneakers
It's fighting the only nature it knows
My mind isn't quite ready to pass the baton
It doesn't want to cross the finish line
It's grown quite comfortable
I'm running through the motions of the race
But neglects to remember
The purpose of the race
Isn't to cross the finish line
But feeling all the emotions
It's who you become on the journey
The real victory
Remains on the inside
My mind was trained in survival mode
Which was only temporary
Not a permanent life sentence
My mind needs some time to catch up
While my heart and body take a breather

Light Forecast

Seeing the light for the first time in a while
Has my eyes burning
Like my heart was cast aside in some file
Has my stomach turning
Like my mouth forgot how to smile
Has my body healing and learning
For him, I would always go the extra mile
Those parts of myself I loved most are returning
His name is special; *it isn't just Kyle*

Fished My Wish

"You should text me sometime"
Without having my number
Was a really good hook
His charm reeled me in
I took his smooth planted bait
Bit off more than I could chew
Plenty of fish in the sea
But in this ocean of blue
I only see him on the line
I drown in his eyes of blue
Stargazing into his soul
I'm taken out of my body
Beamed up into his light
An experience some call
an *alien* abduction
I wasn't taken
But our love is surely
Outer worldly
My heart is not mistaken

Homecoming

There's a lingering in the air
Something I can't quite put my finger on
Something is coming
Someone is moving
Somewhere there's a shift happening
Long drives are becoming more frequent
Recharging is becoming more essential
Spending time with myself is happening more often
They say 'don't trip over what's behind you'
But I'm falling over what's right in front of me
Boxes I have yet to unpack
Sit there staring me in the face
Asking me to open them
Begging to see the light of day
I fear if I open one of them
The floodgates will open
There'll be too much to unpack
Afraid I'll get knocked off track
Distracted from my path

Can't heal in the same environment that made me sick
Yet here I am trying to heal myself
Attempting to unpack these boxes
Where the baggage was born
Time to set sail
Time to flee the nest
Ready to take flight
Ready to spread my wings
I am made of light
Meant to lead by my heartstrings
I've always had true sight
Enough time spent in a house not conducive of growth
Didn't lead to relying on a safety net
But turned these freedom wings
Into a weighted, wet blanket
Heavy on my back
Carry around unnecessary burdens
Time to take my power back
Time to leave this baggage on the stoop
It's time for me to fly the coop

www.ingramcontent.com/pod-product-compliance
Lightning Source LLC
Chambersburg PA
CBHW051001030426
42339CB00007B/438